DEDICATION

To:

Karin Matthews for her strength and grace during the creation of this book. We all stand in agreement with you.

To:

My beautiful wife Cyndi for her dedication and love.

CEPHER PUBLISHING CO.

Cepher Publishing, a subsidiary of Hagios Holding Company, is dedicated to serving the Christian and Family Values marketplace. To this end, Cepher Publishing makes the work of talented writers and artists, with a similar vision, available to the public.

Cepher Publishing Company

10120 Red Oak Drive, Baton Rouge, LA 70815-1628

Hagios.com

Copyright © 1999 by Cepher Publishing Company

All rights reserved. No part of this publication may be reproduced, stored

in a retrieval system, or transmitted in any form or by any means

- electronic, mechanical, photocopy, recording, or any other -

except for brief quotations in printed reviews, without the prior permission

of the publisher.

ISBN 09662913-8-7

Printed and Bound in the United States of America by Inland Press

Proofreading by Angie Bush

Book Design by Keith Neely Design, Inc.

Baton Rouge, LA

Smile, God Loves You!

...and the adventure begins...

Written by Douglas King
Illustrated by Rodney Matthews

...and the adventure begins...

The Snugeldorfs live in the land of Ompadoodle, sharing the land with Dooglebirds that eat the Dooglenoodle, and Wellophants that love to dance, Dimpletrees with Dimpleberries, Wimplewhales with shiny tails, and Scabiesnails with miniature wind sails. There are Bumbliebees that zip about speedily and even Duncklehopper-Apes that eat Duncklehopper-grapes.

The life of a Snugeldorf is a life of work and play. They give thanks to their Creator each and every day.

They love to make music with their googlygong, drums and dinkle-poo. They use their voices as an instrument too. Sometimes they play all day and all night. When the Snugeldorfs play music, you know everything is all right.

There is one thing that the Snugeldorfs do fear, and that is when a Mantupid is near. Big, smelly creatures that are dirty and wasteful, the Snugeldorfs and other animals find them most distasteful. The Mantupid lives in dark, dank caves, which could be the explanation for the way he behaves. They are big and they are stupid. That is a Mantupid.

And so in the land of Ompadoodle, a joyful place where the Snugeldorfs live, the fun is measured in oodles. The happiness is returned in the love they give. You are free to visit here whenever you feel. Please believe me when I say the Snugeldorfs are real. And if you are lucky, they might play you a song. Luckier still, they might invite you to play along.

*A cheerful look brings joy to the heart,
and good news gives health to the bones.*

In the town of Scapipili-pad,
all of the Snugeldorfs were depressed and sad.
Each wore a long face or a frown of discontent.
What they needed was a change of pace
or a blessed event.

The sad were sad
and the mad were mad.
Everyone in Scapipili-pad
felt down right bad.

They grumped and they gloomed.
They frumped and they fumed.
The Snugeldorfs, they did.
Nothing good ever happened to them.
So they said.

Then one fine and sunny day,
when all the townsfolk figured their sadness was there to stay,
along came a traveler, obviously from somewhere far away,
for he sang and he smiled as he walked on his way.
He sang songs of thanksgiving and songs of praise.
He smiled and laughed.
He thanked God for such glorious days.

The traveler's name was Hapaflappadappla-do.
But, his friends call him Hap for short,
and you should too.

On the road entering the town,
Hap came upon a child wearing an awfully big frown.
So Hap tipped his hat and smiled as big as could be,
and the boy smiled back quite amazingly.
For Hap's cheerful look had brought happiness and joy
to the heart of this very young boy.

And the child ran off
and played for the first time,
in a long time,
for it was high time,
in his lifetime,
that he make time,
for playtime.

Hap walked on, smiling
to each and everyone.
He smiled because he was happy.
He smiled because it was fun.
And all whom he smiled at
became filled with good cheer.
And they said, "Well, well, we
welcome you here."

Then Hap moved on, on into the town,
where everyone walked with their faces
turned down.
Hap stepped into the town square where
all would have a view,
and he shouted at the top of his lungs,
"Smile, God loves you."

All that heard him stopped
and did stare.

"Why, this is the best news," they did declare.

It was.

It was.

And, all could share

the fact that God above really did care.

But, there was still one old Snugeldorf who was unhappy.
He was old and cranky.
His name was Flipbingscrappy.
While everyone else sang and danced to the music of the dinkle-poo,
Flipbingscrappy sat on his stool
alone,
to stew.

Hap stopped the singing
and called everyone around.
He made them form a circle.
It was Flipbingscrappy they did surround.
And, Hap had each Snugeldorf smile as
big as big can be,
but Flipbingscrappy just sat there as
if he didn't see.

Then Hap gathered some others to give Flip a hug, which Flipbingscrappy accepted with nothing but a shrug.
To some it seemed as if nothing might work, but Hap knew it would take teamwork, to rework, Flipbingscrappy's saddened brainwork.

So Hap began to praise him and encourage him. The others did too. And, you know, soon a smile began to show through.

Slowly at first,
but soon the feeling grew,
and then Flipbingscrappy said to the crowd,
"Oh, God bless you!"

So, the town was filled with laughter and tears of joy. A smile was on everyone's face, on every Snugeldorf girl and boy. And to this day they remain happy, even good old Flipbingscrappy.

And that's how the
town of Scapipilipad
went from feeling sad to glad.
All they needed was a cheerful smile.
We all need that every once in awhile.

So if you're ever sad
or can't shake being blue,
just remember what the Snugeldorf's do:
wear a smile and sing a song.
And maybe,
just maybe,
Hapaflappadappla-do might come along.